Pages 13, 14 and 20 are missing these handwritten examples. Please refer to these pages for completed information.

HOW TO PRAY

Five important aspects of prayer will help you in your conversation with God. Use these as you talk to Him every day. Then write the results on your PRAYER ACTION SHEET beginning on page 30. The following example will show you how to do this:

PRAYER ACTION SHEET

DAY/DATE __Jan . 24__

PRAISE
Write down one praise to the Lord today:
From Psalm 8: Lord your name is majestic and your name crowned me with glory and honor.

CONFESSION
Write down any sin(s) you need to confess:
Lord, I've struggled with lust, I confess. Forgive me and strengthen me. (2 Tim . 2:22)

THANKSGIVING
Write down what you are most thankful for today:
Thanks for my friend Tony, for my good test grade, and for my parents.

PETITION
Write down any needs you have in your life today:
① to get all of my homework done
② to love Angela when she bugs me
③ to speak to Michael about Jesus today.

INTERCESSION
Write the names of the people you are praying for today and a phrase that expresses your prayer for each person:

Name	Prayer
Mom & Dad	get along better
Angela	come to Christ
Michael	heal broken arm

14

PRAYING FOR OTHERS

 Through your prayers God will work powerfully in other people's lives. Pray for: your family, your Christian friends, friends who need Christ, your school, your church, and the spread of the Gospel around the world. Be very specific in your requests.

Record your prayers on your PRAYER ACTION SHEET beginning on page 30.

Keep a record of the things you are praying for and write down God's answers to your prayers on pages 22–28. Put in request on each day of the week. Then pray for those requests on that day. Doing this will keep you from having too many requests on one day.

SUNDAY

Date Prayed	REQUEST	ANSWER	Date Answered
10/27	MoM – Flu – relationship with sister Dad – new job – growth as Christian Daniel – attitude toward me – girlfriend Susan – grades – discipline – parents' divorce	MoM – out of bed & feeling much better today Susan – parents talking about getting back together	10/28

20

BIBLE RESPONSE SHEET

DAY/DATE **10/27 Monday**

PASSAGE **John 1:1-5**

TITLE (Topic of passage) **Jesus brings light & life**

KEY VERSE **4**

WHAT DOES IT SAY? (Outline) **The Word (Jesus)**

1. was in the beginning

2. was with God

3. was God

4. made all things

5. was life

6. was light

HOW DOES IT APPLY TO MY LIFE? **I need to let Jesus be who He wants to be to me. I can experience His light and Life by spending time alone with Him every morning for the next 30 days.**

MEMORIZE VERSE

13

BARRY ST. CLAIR

TIME ALONE WITH GOD
Notebook

VICTOR BOOKS

A DIVISION OF SCRIPTURE PRESS PUBLICATIONS INC.
USA CANADA ENGLAND

THIS BOOK BELONGS TO...

NAME————————————————

ADDRESS————————————————

————————————————

PHONE————————————————

DATE COMPLETED ————————

ISBN: 1-56476-143-6
© 1993, Barry St. Clair. All rights reserved
Printed in the United States of America
Published by Victor Books, Wheaton, IL 60187

Produced in cooperation with
  Reach Out Ministries
  3961 Holcomb Bridge Road, Suite 201
  Norcross, GA 30092

WHAT'S IN THE NOTEBOOK?

Everyone wants to know, "What is the purpose of my life?" The answer is not complex. The Apostle Paul explains, "Whether, then, you eat or drink or whatever you do, do all to the glory of God" (1 Corinthians 10:31, NASB).

So then how do we glorify God? The answer is found in 2 Corinthians 3:18: "But we Christians have no veil over our faces; we can be mirrors that brightly reflect the glory of the Lord. And as the Spirit of the Lord works within us, we become more and more like him" (TLB).

How, then, do we become more like Him? Luke describes how that took place with the disciples in Acts 4:13, "When the council saw the boldness of Peter and John, and could see that they were obviously uneducated, non-professionals, they were amazed and realized what being with Jesus had done for them!" (TLB)

We need to spend time "being with Jesus" so we can know Him, and become more like Him in our attitudes and actions.

We can spend time with Him in two ways:

1. **Through the Bible:** Hebrews 4:12 says: "The word of God is living and active. Sharper than any double-edged sword, it penetrates even to dividing soul and spirit, joints and marrow; it judges the thoughts and attitudes of the heart."

2. **Through Prayer:** Hebrews 4:16 encourages us: "Let us then approach the throne of grace with confidence, so that we may receive mercy and find grace to help us in our time of need."

Every growing Christian spends time alone with God daily—with no exceptions! From Moses, Abraham, and Billy Graham ... to each of us, time alone with God is the most important single discipline in the Christian life. God wants us to get in on it! We can too, as we put into practice the simple plan on the following pages.

Our hope is that as we begin to spend time alone with God daily, we will know Him, seek Him, and love Him more and more. That's the reason we exist!

WHAT IS TIME ALONE WITH GOD?

In order to encounter God, we need to know what is supposed to happen when we meet Him.

1. We experience fellowship with God. A guy and girl date. How do they get to know each other? By spending time together. And some of the best times together are times alone! We get to know Jesus Christ the same way we get to know a person we date—by spending time alone with Him.

The whole purpose of the Christian life is getting to know Jesus Christ, according to the Apostle Paul. In Philippians 3:10 he says, "that I may know Him."

Spending Time Alone with God helps us get to know Jesus in a personal and intimate way.

2. We ask God to speak to us about our lives. At school, on the job, or at home we rush all day long—class to class, friend to friend, home to homework. Then we hit the sack exhausted.

Rarely do we take an honest look at ourselves to find out who we really are. But God wants us to say with the psalmist: "Search me, O God, and know my heart; test me and know my anxious thoughts. See if there is any offensive way in me, and lead me in the way everlasting" (Psalm 139:23-24).

A time alone with God lets us see ourselves through the eyes of Jesus. It is not preparing our lessons, daydreaming, or reading the newspaper. It is when God shows us how we need to be like Jesus—pointing out sins in our lives, helping us to admit those sins, and giving us power to do something about them. And then, as we look at ourselves in light of His Word, we see how we can become like Jesus.

3. We commit our day to the Lord. Think about all of the things coming up for the day—a test, a party, an appointment, shopping, ball practice, band, a date. Give those things to Christ and trust Him to take care of them. Proverbs 3:5-6 encourages us to, "Trust in the Lord with all of your heart, and do not rely on your own insight. In all your ways acknowledge him and he will make straight your paths." When we wake up in the morning, we can invite Jesus to guide us through the day. Luke 9:23 says, "Take up your cross daily." That means that we give up our desires in order that He might live through us daily.

We will be motivated to spend time alone with God when we understand why it is so important.

1. God desires our fellowship. Now that is a staggering thought! The God who made the stars, seas, ants, and babies gets joy, satisfaction, and pleasure from being with us! That's amazing!

Often people read the Bible and pray because they have to or because they should, or they just don't do it at all. But the exciting truth is that God wants us to read His Word and talk to Him because He likes to be around us. And we will enjoy Him too. When we are with Him, He "makes our joy complete" (1 John 1:4).

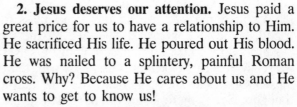

2. Jesus deserves our attention. Jesus paid a great price for us to have a relationship to Him. He sacrificed His life. He poured out His blood. He was nailed to a splintery, painful Roman cross. Why? Because He cares about us and He wants to get to know us!

When we are alone with God, we take our eyes off ourselves and focus our eyes on Him. He is more than worthy of our praise, our adoration, our love, and our life. He deserves our attention!

3. The Holy Spirit gives us a daily relationship. How many times have we come back from a camp or a conference high as a kite, then from two days to six months later—bam! We fall flat on our faces. And so we are out of it spiritually until the next camp or conference. After several times we begin to think: "This 'Jesus Christ business' does not work anyway."

The problem is that we had not developed a *daily* relationship with Christ.

Jesus had a need for daily fellowship with His Father. The Gospel of Mark says, "And in the morning, a great while before day, he rose and went out to a lonely place, and there he prayed" (Mark 1:35). Jesus was alone with His Father often. If it was that important for Jesus, then how much more important is it for us?

6

HOW TO HAVE A
TIME ALONE WITH GOD

When we have made these practical decisions about time alone with God, we are ready to begin.

1. Choose a time. Have you ever been stood-up on a date? Or have you had an appointment fall through? It's frustrating. God feels the same way. We need to make a date with the Lord. We commit ourselves to God at a certain time each day and then do not stand Him up!

The best time to meet Him is in the morning. The psalmist says, "Let me see your kindness to me in the morning" (Psalm 143:8). Have you ever seen a football team warm up after the game? Have you ever heard a symphony warm up after the concert? In the morning we are fresh (after a shower) and the day is ahead of us. God desires and deserves the best time in our day.

Would you commit yourself to a 15-minute time alone with God every morning for one month?

➡ *Fill out the personal commitment on page 9.*

2. Choose a place. We need to pick a definite place to meet God. That's what the great man of God, Abraham, did. "That morning Abraham was up early and hurried out to the place where he stood before the Lord" (Genesis 19:27).

Look for a quiet place where you can be alone with God without distractions or interruptions—your room, your basement, or some other quiet place.

➡ *Write here the place you have chosen* _____

3. Choose an attitude. Attitude is everything. Decide to pursue God with these attitudes.

Meet God with a *quiet intensity*. We don't come to our time alone with God like a bird in a hurricane, or like a fan at the Super Bowl. We come to God quietly and reverently. Psalm 46:10 instructs us: "Be still and know that I am God." But do not come so quietly that you fall asleep. We need to be alert and awake. Do some exercises if necessary. Remember, we are meeting the Living God.

Expect God's presence. We need to expect Him to do something as we expose ourselves to His Spirit. The psalmist says, "You will fill me with joy in your presence" (Psalm 16:11). He wants to do the same for us as we meet Him every day.

Set your goal. The objective of our time alone with God is to get to know Jesus Christ. As we focus on Jesus, He will change us to be like Him. That is the promise of Romans 8:29: "For from the very beginning God decided that those who came to Him—and all along He knew who would—should become like His Son, so that His Son would be the first, with many brothers" (TLB). Our objective is clear!

➤ *I want my attitude to be* _____

4. Choose a plan. A balanced time alone with God includes Bible study, praise, thanksgiving, confession, petition, and intercession. The guideline below includes all aspects of Bible reading and prayer within a 15- to 20-minute period of time each day. Expand the time you spend alone with God after it has become a daily habit.

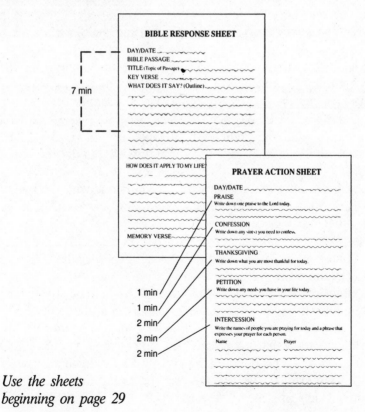

Use the sheets
beginning on page 29

PERSONAL COMMITMENT

Because I want to get to know Jesus better,

I, _____
                    (name)

agree to have a daily time alone with God at

_____ and at _____
           (place)   (time)

for _____ days.

Signature _____

Date _____

PRACTICAL SUGGESTIONS FOR
TIME ALONE WITH GOD

These tested ideas will make our time alone with God better.

1. Use this notebook. Use it not only for time alone with God, but for sermon notes, ideas, a journal, and study. (You will find blank sheets for this at the back of this book.)

2. Go to bed on time. It is impossible to stay up late and then wake up fresh the next day. Set a date with the Lord, then go to bed in order to wake up on time.

3. Get up in the morning. This takes discipline! How can you make it easier to get up?
- Pray the night before about getting up.
- Exercise will power. Once up, stay up.
- Get wide-awake before meeting with the Lord. Exercise and shower if necessary.
- Stand up or walk if sleep attacks you.

4. Focus on Jesus. Let your first conscious thoughts focus on Jesus. As soon as you wake up, kneel beside your bed and talk to the Lord.

5. Keep going. If you miss a morning, do not worry about it. You will not be a failure if you miss a day. Just don't miss the next day.

6. Be honest. If you feel your time alone with God is empty and worthless, tell the Lord about it honestly. Claim the promise of His presence. Don't quit! He will honor your time with Him apart from your feelings.

7. Be consistent. Some days you will have a great time. Some days it will be rather routine. Either way, you will grow by spending time with the Lord every day.

Remember that what Jeremiah said so long ago is true for you right now: "You will seek me and find me; when you seek me with all your heart, I will be found by you, says the Lord" (Jeremiah 29:13-14).

HOW TO STUDY A
PASSAGE OF SCRIPTURE

Follow these steps to make Bible study exciting. Use them on the BIBLE RESPONSE SHEETS starting on page 29.

Observe. (Use with the *Title* and *Key Verse* sections of the BIBLE RESPONSE SHEET.)

Pray first for the Holy Spirit's guidance and then read the passage carefully. Read with an open mind, ready to receive and obey what God has to teach you.

Interpret. (Use with the *What does it say?* section of the BIBLE RESPONSE SHEET.)

Step One — Read the verses preceding and following the passage in order to understand the proper setting and context.

Step Two — Look up unfamiliar terms in a standard dictionary or a Bible dictionary.

Step Three — Outline the passage.

Apply. (Use with the *How does it apply to my life?* section of the BIBLE RESPONSE SHEET.)

Step One — Look for:

Promises to claim	Commands to obey
Attitudes to change	Actions to take
Challenges to accept	Examples to follow
Sins to confess	Skills to learn

Step Two — Describe how the passage applies to your life by asking yourself these questions:

- "How can I make this passage *personal?*"
- "How can I make it *practical?*"
- "How can I make it *measurable?*"

Be specific. For example: "I need to love my mom more by cleaning up my room every day."

Memorize. (Use the *Memory verse* section of the BIBLE RESPONSE SHEET.)

Find a verse or passage of Scripture that speaks to you personally and memorize it. You will find specific steps to Scripture memory on the next page.

These steps will make Scripture memorization a fun experience.

Read the passage several times.
First read it silently and then aloud.

Understand the passage.
➡ Read it in the context of the passages around it.
➡ Read the comments about the verse in a Bible commentary (for example, *Wycliffe Bible Commentary*) or a good study Bible.
➡ Write in a few words explaining what the passage is about.

Visualize the passage. Use your imagination to picture the passage. For example, Matthew 5:1-12 is part of the "Sermon on the Mount." Picture yourself there on the mountain with Jesus. Then place each of these "Beatitudes" on the side of the mountain. Later, that picture will come to mind and help you recall these verses.

Break down the passage into natural phrases. Learn the first phrase of the passage, then add the second. Continue adding phrases until you have memorized the entire passage.

Learn the reference as part of the passage. Say the reference, then the verse, then repeat the reference again at the end. This step helps you fix the location of the verse in your mind, allowing you to turn to it immediately when you need it.

Learn it word perfect. As you say the passage over and over to yourself, continue to correct yourself until you have learned it exactly as it is written. You are already taking the time to learn it, so why not do it right? Learning it this way now will give you confidence to quote the passage later.

Meditate on the passage. As you think and pray about the passage, ask God to speak to you. When the passage becomes meaningful to you, then it will be much easier for you to remember.

Review the passage. Each day, review the Scripture passages you have already learned. If you review a passage every day for 30 days, it will be very difficult to forget.

BIBLE RESPONSE SHEET

DAY/DATE ⎯⎯⎯⎯⎯⎯⎯⎯⎯⎯⎯⎯

PASSAGE ⎯⎯⎯⎯⎯⎯⎯⎯⎯⎯⎯⎯

TITLE (Topic of passage) ⎯⎯⎯⎯⎯⎯

⎯⎯⎯⎯⎯⎯⎯⎯⎯⎯⎯⎯⎯⎯⎯⎯

KEY VERSE ⎯⎯⎯⎯⎯⎯⎯⎯⎯⎯⎯⎯

WHAT DOES IT SAY? (Outline) ⎯⎯⎯⎯⎯

⎯⎯⎯⎯⎯⎯⎯⎯⎯⎯⎯⎯⎯⎯⎯⎯

⎯⎯⎯⎯⎯⎯⎯⎯⎯⎯⎯⎯⎯⎯⎯⎯

⎯⎯⎯⎯⎯⎯⎯⎯⎯⎯⎯⎯⎯⎯⎯⎯

⎯⎯⎯⎯⎯⎯⎯⎯⎯⎯⎯⎯⎯⎯⎯⎯

⎯⎯⎯⎯⎯⎯⎯⎯⎯⎯⎯⎯⎯⎯⎯⎯

HOW DOES IT APPLY TO MY LIFE? ⎯⎯⎯⎯

⎯⎯⎯⎯⎯⎯⎯⎯⎯⎯⎯⎯⎯⎯⎯⎯

⎯⎯⎯⎯⎯⎯⎯⎯⎯⎯⎯⎯⎯⎯⎯⎯

⎯⎯⎯⎯⎯⎯⎯⎯⎯⎯⎯⎯⎯⎯⎯⎯

⎯⎯⎯⎯⎯⎯⎯⎯⎯⎯⎯⎯⎯⎯⎯⎯

⎯⎯⎯⎯⎯⎯⎯⎯⎯⎯⎯⎯⎯⎯⎯⎯

⎯⎯⎯⎯⎯⎯⎯⎯⎯⎯⎯⎯⎯⎯⎯⎯

MEMORIZE VERSE ⎯⎯⎯⎯⎯⎯⎯⎯⎯⎯

⎯⎯⎯⎯⎯⎯⎯⎯⎯⎯⎯⎯⎯⎯⎯⎯

HOW TO PRAY

Five important aspects of prayer will help you in your conversation with God. Use these as you talk to Him every day. Then write the results on your PRAYER ACTION SHEET beginning on page 30. The following example will show you how to do this:

PRAYER ACTION SHEET

DAY/DATE_____

PRAISE
Write down one praise to the Lord today:

_____

_____

CONFESSION
Write down any sin(s) you need to confess:

_____

_____

THANKSGIVING
Write down what you are most thankful for today:

_____

_____

PETITION
Write down any needs you have in your life today:

_____

_____

INTERCESSION
Write the names of the people you are praying for today and a phrase that expresses your prayer for each person:

Name   Prayer

_____   _____

_____   _____

_____   _____

NEEDS IN MY LIFE

As you pray:
  (1) Keep a record of the things you are pray-
      ing for and
  (2) Write down God's answers to those prayers.

Date Prayed	REQUEST	ANSWER	Date Answered

THIRTY DAYS OF PRAISE

Read a psalm. Address it to the Lord. Read it aloud. Praise the Lord for who He is. Record it on your PRAYER ACTION SHEET beginning on page 30.

Day 1: Psalm 8
Day 2: Psalm 23
Day 3: Psalms 24:1-3; 50:1-6
Day 4: Psalms 63:1-4; 66:1-7
Day 5: Psalm 67
Day 6: Psalm 84
Day 7: Psalm 86
Day 8: Psalm 90
Day 9: Psalm 91
Day 10: Psalm 92
Day 11: Psalm 93
Day 12: Psalm 95:1-7
Day 13: Psalm 96
Day 14: Psalm 100
Day 15: Psalm 103

Day 16: Psalm 104:1-23
Day 17: Psalm 104:24-35
Day 18: Psalm 111
Day 19: Psalm 112
Day 20: Psalm 113
Day 21: Psalm 134
Day 22: Psalm 135:1-7
Day 23: Psalm 138
Day 24: Psalm 139
Day 25: Psalm 145
Day 26: Psalm 146
Day 27: Psalm 147
Day 28: Psalm 148
Day 29: Psalm 149
Day 30: Psalm 150

Search your heart. Think of specific instances of sin(s) you need to confess. Admit your sin to God. Claim His promise of forgiveness in 1 John 1:9, "If we confess our sins, He is faithful and just and will forgive us our sins and purify us from all unrighteousness." Record your confession on your PRAYER ACTION SHEET beginning on page 30.

Sins to Confess:

Day 1: 2 Timothy 2:22. Do I have impure thoughts?
Day 2: Philippians 2:14-15. Do I complain or gripe?
Day 3: Ephesians 6:1-3. Do I honor my parents?
Day 4: Ephesians 4:31. Am I bitter toward anyone?
Day 5: 1 Corinthians 6:19-20. Am I careless with my body?
Day 6: Matthew 6:33. Do I seek what God wants first?
Day 7: Matthew 6:14. Do I have a bad attitude toward someone?
Day 8: 2 Timothy 2:22. Do I have impure motives?
Day 9: Colossians 3:9. Do I lie?
Day 10: Ephesians 6:1-3. Do I respect my parents?
Day 11: Ephesians 4:31. Is there anger in my life?
Day 12: 1 Corinthians 6:19-20. Do I have bad habits?
Day 13: Matthew 6:33. Is God the most important person in my life?
Day 14: Matthew 6:14. Am I holding a grudge?
Day 15: 2 Timothy 2:22. Are my thoughts pure toward the opposite sex?
Day 16: Philippians 2:14-15. Do I have a critical attitude?
Day 17: Colossians 3:9. Do I steal?
Day 18: Ephesians 4:31. Do I talk about others behind their backs?
Day 19: 1 Corinthians 6:19-20. Am I lazy?
Day 20: Matthew 6:33. Have I given God everything in my life?
Day 21: Matthew 6:14. Do I have a wrong relationship with someone?
Day 22: Colossians 3:9. Do I cheat in school?
Day 23: Ephesians 6:1-3. Do I have problems with authority?
Day 24: Ephesians 4:31. Am I jealous of anyone?
Day 25: 1 Corinthians 6:19-20. Do I eat too much?
Day 26: Matthew 6:33. Am I trusting God with my life?
Day 27: Matthew 6:14. Is there anyone I resent?
Day 28: Philippians 2:14-15. Does my attitude honor God?
Day 29: Ephesians 6:1-3. Am I rebellious?
Day 30: Ephesians 4:31. Do I argue with other people?

THIRTY DAYS OF THANKSGIVING

Thank God for all of the circumstances of your life. First Thessalonians 5:18 tells why it is important to thank Him for the good and the bad, "Give thanks in all circumstances, for this is God's will for you in Christ Jesus." Record your expressions of thanks on your PRAYER ACTION SHEET beginning on page 30. Focus your thanks to the Lord through these promises each day. Pray these promises back to God as an expression of thanks. For example:

- Pray through 2 Peter 1:4 to express your thanks to God.
- Pray, "Lord, thank You for Your great and precious promises that You have given to me that I might be part of Your divine nature."

Then, as you think back on the previous day, thank God for what He has done.

Promises to claim:

Day 1: Philippians 4:8

Day 2: Psalm 119:9

Day 3: Colossians 3:9-10

Day 4: Galatians 2:20

Day 5: Colossians 3:20

Day 6: 1 John 4:7

Day 7: Hebrews 12:15

Day 8: Ephesians 4:29

Day 9: 1 Corinthians 6:13

Day 10: Colossians 1:27

Day 11: Luke 9:23

Day 12: 2 Corinthians 9:8

Day 13: 1 John 4:4

Day 14: Philippians 1:9

Day 15: 2 Thessalonians 1:12

Day 16: 1 Corinthians 10:13

Day 17: 1 Thessalonians 4:3

Day 18: Ephesians 2:10

Day 19: Colossians 1:13

Day 20: Ephesians 6:2

Day 21: Galatians 5:18

Day 22: Ephesians 4:26

Day 23: 1 Corinthians 3:16

Day 24: Romans 12:1

Day 25: 2 Corinthians 5:17

Day 26: Philippians 2:5-7

Day 27: Matthew 6:12

Day 28: Ephesians 1:3-7

Day 29: Colossians 2:2-3

Day 30: Philippians 3:1

Ask God for what you need. His desire is to give you what He knows you need. He made a promise to you about that in John 15:7: "If you remain in Me and My words remain in you, ask whatever you wish, and it will be given you." Record your petitions on your PRAYER ACTION SHEET beginning on page 30.

Focus your petitions in two areas each day:
(1) Bible passages that describe what God wants for you. Promises to claim daily. For example:

> **Sunday**
> Read Galatians 2:20
>
> **Monday**
> Read Galatians 5:22-23
>
> **Tuesday**
> Read Ephesians 5:18
>
> **Wednesday**
> Read 1 Corinthians 12:4-6
>
> **Thursday**
> Read Ephesians 6:10-11
>
> **Friday**
> Read Isaiah 41:10
>
> **Saturday**
> Read Acts 1:8

(2) Your personal requests for God to supply your needs. Record your personal requests and answers on the "Needs in My Life" pages. Then each day, as you pray, jot down the prayers you are praying for that day on the PRAYER ACTION SHEET.

Through your prayers God will work powerfully in other people's lives. Pray for: your family, your Christian friends, friends who need Christ, your school, your church, and the spread of the Gospel around the world. Be very specific in your requests.

Record your prayers on your PRAYER ACTION SHEET beginning on page 30.

Keep a record of the things you are praying for and write down God's answers to your prayers on pages 22–28. Put in request on each day of the week. Then pray for those requests on that day. Doing this will keep you from having too many requests on one day.

SUNDAY

Date Prayed	REQUEST	ANSWER	Date Answered

Look at these prayers of the Apostle Paul. They will help you know how to pray for other people. In fact, you can pray these specific prayers for them.

Romans 10:1: "Brothers, my heart's desire and prayer to God for them is that they may be saved."

Colossians 1:9-11: "For this reason, since the day we heard about you, we have not stopped praying for you and asking God to fill you with the knowledge of his will through all spiritual wisdom and understanding. And we pray this in order that you may live a life worthy of the Lord and may please him in every way bearing fruit in every good work, growing in the knowledge of God, being strengthened with all power according to his glorious might so that you may have great endurance and patience."

Philippians 1:9-11: "And this is my prayer: that your love may abound more and more in knowledge and depth of insight, so that you may be able to discern what is best and may be pure and blameless until the day of Christ, filled with the fruit of righteousness that comes through Jesus Christ—to the glory and praise of God."

Ephesians 1:17: "I keep asking that the God of our Lord Jesus Christ, the glorious Father, may give you the Spirit of wisdom and revelation, so that you may know him better."

Ephesians 1:18-19: "I pray also that the eyes of your heart may be enlightened in order that you may know the hope to which he has called you, the riches of his glorious inheritance in the saints, and his incomparably great power for us who believe. That power is like the working of his mighty strength."

Ephesians 3:16-19: "I pray that out of His glorious riches He may strengthen you with power through his Spirit in your inner being so that Christ may dwell in your hearts through faith. And I pray that you, being rooted and established in love, may have power, together with all the saints, to grasp how wide and long and high and deep is the love of Christ, and to know this love that surpasses knowledge— that you may be filled to the measure of all the fullness of God."

SUNDAY

Date Prayed	REQUEST	ANSWER	Date Answered

Date Prayed	REQUEST	ANSWER	Date Answered

Date Prayed	REQUEST	ANSWER	Date Answered

WEDNESDAY

Date Prayed	REQUEST	ANSWER	Date Answered

Date Prayed	REQUEST	ANSWER	Date Answered

FRIDAY

Date Prayed	REQUEST	ANSWER	Date Answered

SATURDAY

Date Prayed	REQUEST	ANSWER	Date Answered

BIBLE RESPONSE SHEET

DAY/DATE_____

PASSAGE_____

TITLE (Topic of passage) _____

_____

KEY VERSE_____

WHAT DOES IT SAY? (Outline) _____

_____

_____

_____

_____

_____

HOW DOES IT APPLY TO MY LIFE? _____

_____

_____

_____

_____

_____

_____

MEMORIZE VERSE_____

_____

PRAYER ACTION SHEET

DAY/DATE_____

PRAISE
Write down one praise to the Lord today:

_____

_____

CONFESSION
Write down any sin(s) you need to confess:

_____

_____

THANKSGIVING
Write down what you are most thankful for today:

_____

_____

PETITION
Write down any needs you have in your life today:

_____

_____

INTERCESSION
Write the names of the people you are praying for today and a
phrase that expresses your prayer for each person:

Name   Prayer

_____   _____

_____   _____

_____   _____

_____   _____

BIBLE RESPONSE SHEET

DAY/DATE _____

PASSAGE _____

TITLE (Topic of passage) _____

_____

KEY VERSE _____

WHAT DOES IT SAY? (Outline) _____

_____

_____

_____

_____

_____

_____

HOW DOES IT APPLY TO MY LIFE? _____

_____

_____

_____

_____

_____

_____

_____

MEMORIZE VERSE _____

_____

PRAYER ACTION SHEET

DAY/DATE_____

PRAISE
Write down one praise to the Lord today:

_____

_____

CONFESSION
Write down any sin(s) you need to confess:

_____

_____

THANKSGIVING
Write down what you are most thankful for today:

_____

_____

PETITION
Write down any needs you have in your life today:

_____

_____

INTERCESSION
Write the names of the people you are praying for today and a phrase that expresses your prayer for each person:

Name   Prayer

_____   _____

_____   _____

_____   _____

_____   _____

BIBLE RESPONSE SHEET

DAY/DATE _____

PASSAGE _____

TITLE (Topic of passage) _____

_____

KEY VERSE _____

WHAT DOES IT SAY? (Outline) _____

_____

_____

_____

_____

_____

_____

HOW DOES IT APPLY TO MY LIFE? _____

_____

_____

_____

_____

_____

_____

_____

MEMORIZE VERSE _____

_____

PRAYER ACTION SHEET

DAY/DATE_____

PRAISE
Write down one praise to the Lord today:

_____

_____

CONFESSION
Write down any sin(s) you need to confess:

_____

_____

THANKSGIVING
Write down what you are most thankful for today:

_____

_____

PETITION
Write down any needs you have in your life today:

_____

_____

INTERCESSION
Write the names of the people you are praying for today and a
phrase that expresses your prayer for each person:

Name   Prayer

_____   _____

_____   _____

_____   _____

_____   _____

BIBLE RESPONSE SHEET

DAY/DATE _____

PASSAGE _____

TITLE (Topic of passage) _____

_____

KEY VERSE _____

WHAT DOES IT SAY? (Outline) _____

_____

_____

_____

_____

_____

HOW DOES IT APPLY TO MY LIFE? _____

_____

_____

_____

_____

_____

_____

MEMORIZE VERSE _____

_____

PRAYER ACTION SHEET

DAY/DATE_____

PRAISE
Write down one praise to the Lord today:

_____

_____

CONFESSION
Write down any sin(s) you need to confess:

_____

_____

THANKSGIVING
Write down what you are most thankful for today:

_____

_____

PETITION
Write down any needs you have in your life today:

_____

_____

INTERCESSION
Write the names of the people you are praying for today and a phrase that expresses your prayer for each person:

Name   Prayer

_____   _____

_____   _____

_____   _____

_____   _____

BIBLE RESPONSE SHEET

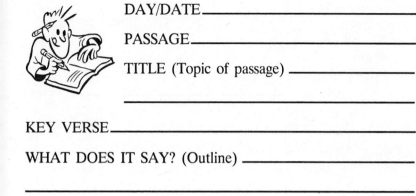

DAY/DATE————————————

PASSAGE————————————

TITLE (Topic of passage) —————————

————————————————

KEY VERSE————————————————

WHAT DOES IT SAY? (Outline) ——————————

————————————————

————————————————

————————————————

————————————————

————————————————

HOW DOES IT APPLY TO MY LIFE? ——————————

————————————————

————————————————

————————————————

————————————————

————————————————

————————————————

MEMORIZE VERSE————————————

————————————————

PRAYER ACTION SHEET

DAY/DATE_____

PRAISE
Write down one praise to the Lord today:

_____

_____

CONFESSION
Write down any sin(s) you need to confess:

_____

_____

THANKSGIVING
Write down what you are most thankful for today:

_____

_____

PETITION
Write down any needs you have in your life today:

_____

_____

INTERCESSION
Write the names of the people you are praying for today and a phrase that expresses your prayer for each person:

Name   Prayer

_____   _____

_____   _____

_____   _____

_____   _____

BIBLE RESPONSE SHEET

DAY/DATE _____

PASSAGE _____

TITLE (Topic of passage) _____

_____

KEY VERSE _____

WHAT DOES IT SAY? (Outline) _____

_____

_____

_____

_____

_____

_____

HOW DOES IT APPLY TO MY LIFE? _____

_____

_____

_____

_____

_____

_____

_____

MEMORIZE VERSE _____

_____

PRAYER ACTION SHEET

DAY/DATE_____

PRAISE
Write down one praise to the Lord today:

_____

_____

CONFESSION
Write down any sin(s) you need to confess:

_____

_____

THANKSGIVING
Write down what you are most thankful for today:

_____

_____

PETITION
Write down any needs you have in your life today:

_____

_____

INTERCESSION
Write the names of the people you are praying for today and a
phrase that expresses your prayer for each person:

Name   Prayer

_____   _____

_____   _____

_____   _____

_____   _____

BIBLE RESPONSE SHEET

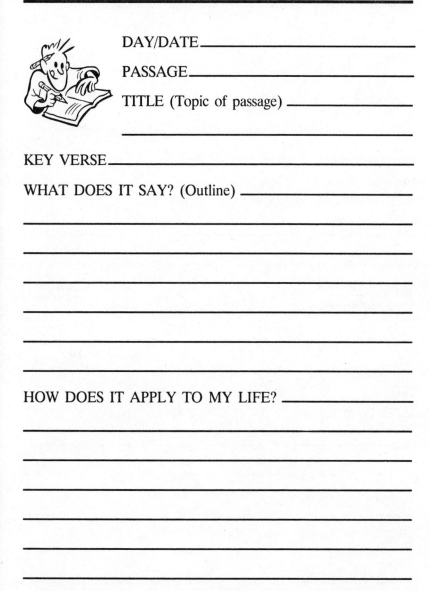

DAY/DATE _____

PASSAGE _____

TITLE (Topic of passage) _____

_____

KEY VERSE _____

WHAT DOES IT SAY? (Outline) _____

_____

_____

_____

_____

_____

_____

HOW DOES IT APPLY TO MY LIFE? _____

_____

_____

_____

_____

_____

_____

_____

MEMORIZE VERSE _____

_____

PRAYER ACTION SHEET

DAY/DATE _____

PRAISE
Write down one praise to the Lord today:

_____

_____

CONFESSION
Write down any sin(s) you need to confess:

_____

_____

THANKSGIVING
Write down what you are most thankful for today:

_____

_____

PETITION
Write down any needs you have in your life today:

_____

_____

INTERCESSION
Write the names of the people you are praying for today and a phrase that expresses your prayer for each person:

Name   Prayer

_____   _____

_____   _____

_____   _____

_____   _____

BIBLE RESPONSE SHEET

DAY/DATE _____

PASSAGE _____

TITLE (Topic of passage) _____

_____

KEY VERSE _____

WHAT DOES IT SAY? (Outline) _____

_____

_____

_____

_____

_____

_____

HOW DOES IT APPLY TO MY LIFE? _____

_____

_____

_____

_____

_____

_____

MEMORIZE VERSE _____

_____

PRAYER ACTION SHEET

DAY/DATE _____

PRAISE
Write down one praise to the Lord today:

_____

_____

CONFESSION
Write down any sin(s) you need to confess:

_____

_____

THANKSGIVING
Write down what you are most thankful for today:

_____

_____

PETITION
Write down any needs you have in your life today:

_____

_____

INTERCESSION
Write the names of the people you are praying for today and a phrase that expresses your prayer for each person:

Name   Prayer

_____   _____

_____   _____

_____   _____

_____   _____

BIBLE RESPONSE SHEET

DAY/DATE_____

PASSAGE_____

TITLE (Topic of passage) _____

_____

KEY VERSE_____

WHAT DOES IT SAY? (Outline) _____

_____

_____

_____

_____

_____

_____

HOW DOES IT APPLY TO MY LIFE? _____

_____

_____

_____

_____

_____

_____

_____

MEMORIZE VERSE_____

_____

PRAYER ACTION SHEET

DAY/DATE _____

PRAISE
Write down one praise to the Lord today:

_____

_____

CONFESSION
Write down any sin(s) you need to confess:

_____

_____

THANKSGIVING
Write down what you are most thankful for today:

_____

_____

PETITION
Write down any needs you have in your life today:

_____

_____

INTERCESSION
Write the names of the people you are praying for today and a phrase that expresses your prayer for each person:

Name   Prayer

_____   _____

_____   _____

_____   _____

_____   _____

BIBLE RESPONSE SHEET

DAY/DATE _____

PASSAGE _____

TITLE (Topic of passage) _____

_____

KEY VERSE _____

WHAT DOES IT SAY? (Outline) _____

_____

_____

_____

_____

_____

_____

HOW DOES IT APPLY TO MY LIFE? _____

_____

_____

_____

_____

_____

_____

_____

MEMORIZE VERSE _____

_____

PRAYER ACTION SHEET

DAY/DATE _____

PRAISE
Write down one praise to the Lord today:

_____

_____

CONFESSION
Write down any sin(s) you need to confess:

_____

_____

THANKSGIVING
Write down what you are most thankful for today:

_____

_____

PETITION
Write down any needs you have in your life today:

_____

_____

INTERCESSION
Write the names of the people you are praying for today and a phrase that expresses your prayer for each person:

Name   Prayer

_____   _____

_____   _____

_____   _____

_____   _____

BIBLE RESPONSE SHEET

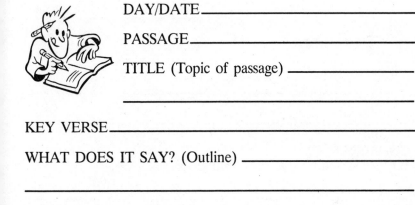

DAY/DATE ⎯⎯⎯⎯⎯⎯⎯⎯⎯⎯

PASSAGE ⎯⎯⎯⎯⎯⎯⎯⎯⎯⎯

TITLE (Topic of passage) ⎯⎯⎯⎯⎯⎯

⎯⎯⎯⎯⎯⎯⎯⎯⎯⎯⎯⎯⎯⎯⎯⎯

KEY VERSE ⎯⎯⎯⎯⎯⎯⎯⎯⎯⎯⎯⎯⎯

WHAT DOES IT SAY? (Outline) ⎯⎯⎯⎯⎯⎯⎯⎯

⎯⎯⎯⎯⎯⎯⎯⎯⎯⎯⎯⎯⎯⎯⎯⎯⎯⎯⎯⎯

⎯⎯⎯⎯⎯⎯⎯⎯⎯⎯⎯⎯⎯⎯⎯⎯⎯⎯⎯⎯

⎯⎯⎯⎯⎯⎯⎯⎯⎯⎯⎯⎯⎯⎯⎯⎯⎯⎯⎯⎯

⎯⎯⎯⎯⎯⎯⎯⎯⎯⎯⎯⎯⎯⎯⎯⎯⎯⎯⎯⎯

⎯⎯⎯⎯⎯⎯⎯⎯⎯⎯⎯⎯⎯⎯⎯⎯⎯⎯⎯⎯

⎯⎯⎯⎯⎯⎯⎯⎯⎯⎯⎯⎯⎯⎯⎯⎯⎯⎯⎯⎯

HOW DOES IT APPLY TO MY LIFE? ⎯⎯⎯⎯⎯⎯

⎯⎯⎯⎯⎯⎯⎯⎯⎯⎯⎯⎯⎯⎯⎯⎯⎯⎯⎯⎯

⎯⎯⎯⎯⎯⎯⎯⎯⎯⎯⎯⎯⎯⎯⎯⎯⎯⎯⎯⎯

⎯⎯⎯⎯⎯⎯⎯⎯⎯⎯⎯⎯⎯⎯⎯⎯⎯⎯⎯⎯

⎯⎯⎯⎯⎯⎯⎯⎯⎯⎯⎯⎯⎯⎯⎯⎯⎯⎯⎯⎯

⎯⎯⎯⎯⎯⎯⎯⎯⎯⎯⎯⎯⎯⎯⎯⎯⎯⎯⎯⎯

⎯⎯⎯⎯⎯⎯⎯⎯⎯⎯⎯⎯⎯⎯⎯⎯⎯⎯⎯⎯

MEMORIZE VERSE ⎯⎯⎯⎯⎯⎯⎯⎯⎯⎯⎯

⎯⎯⎯⎯⎯⎯⎯⎯⎯⎯⎯⎯⎯⎯⎯⎯⎯⎯⎯⎯

PRAYER ACTION SHEET

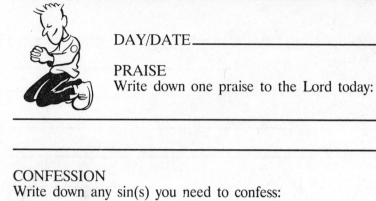

DAY/DATE_____

PRAISE
Write down one praise to the Lord today:

_____

_____

CONFESSION
Write down any sin(s) you need to confess:

_____

_____

THANKSGIVING
Write down what you are most thankful for today:

_____

_____

PETITION
Write down any needs you have in your life today:

_____

_____

INTERCESSION
Write the names of the people you are praying for today and a phrase that expresses your prayer for each person:

Name   Prayer

_____   _____

_____   _____

_____   _____

_____   _____

BIBLE RESPONSE SHEET

DAY/DATE

PASSAGE

TITLE (Topic of passage)

KEY VERSE

WHAT DOES IT SAY? (Outline)

HOW DOES IT APPLY TO MY LIFE?

MEMORIZE VERSE

PRAYER ACTION SHEET

DAY/DATE_____

PRAISE
Write down one praise to the Lord today:

_____

_____

CONFESSION
Write down any sin(s) you need to confess:

_____

_____

THANKSGIVING
Write down what you are most thankful for today:

_____

_____

PETITION
Write down any needs you have in your life today:

_____

_____

INTERCESSION
Write the names of the people you are praying for today and a phrase that expresses your prayer for each person:

Name   Prayer

_____   _____

_____   _____

_____   _____

_____   _____

BIBLE RESPONSE SHEET

DAY/DATE _____

PASSAGE _____

TITLE (Topic of passage) _____

_____

KEY VERSE _____

WHAT DOES IT SAY? (Outline) _____

_____

_____

_____

_____

_____

HOW DOES IT APPLY TO MY LIFE? _____

_____

_____

_____

_____

_____

MEMORIZE VERSE _____

_____

PRAYER ACTION SHEET

DAY/DATE_____

PRAISE
Write down one praise to the Lord today:

_____

_____

CONFESSION
Write down any sin(s) you need to confess:

_____

_____

THANKSGIVING
Write down what you are most thankful for today:

_____

_____

PETITION
Write down any needs you have in your life today:

_____

_____

INTERCESSION
Write the names of the people you are praying for today and a
phrase that expresses your prayer for each person:

Name   Prayer

_____   _____

_____   _____

_____   _____

_____   _____

BIBLE RESPONSE SHEET

DAY/DATE_____

PASSAGE_____

TITLE (Topic of passage) _____

_____

KEY VERSE_____

WHAT DOES IT SAY? (Outline) _____

_____

_____

_____

_____

_____

HOW DOES IT APPLY TO MY LIFE? _____

_____

_____

_____

_____

_____

MEMORIZE VERSE_____

_____

PRAYER ACTION SHEET

DAY/DATE _____

PRAISE
Write down one praise to the Lord today:

_____

_____

CONFESSION
Write down any sin(s) you need to confess:

_____

_____

THANKSGIVING
Write down what you are most thankful for today:

_____

_____

PETITION
Write down any needs you have in your life today:

_____

_____

INTERCESSION
Write the names of the people you are praying for today and a
phrase that expresses your prayer for each person:

Name   Prayer

_____   _____

_____   _____

_____   _____

_____   _____

BIBLE RESPONSE SHEET

DAY/DATE _____

PASSAGE _____

TITLE (Topic of passage) _____

_____

KEY VERSE _____

WHAT DOES IT SAY? (Outline) _____

_____

_____

_____

_____

_____

_____

HOW DOES IT APPLY TO MY LIFE? _____

_____

_____

_____

_____

_____

_____

_____

MEMORIZE VERSE _____

_____

PRAYER ACTION SHEET

DAY/DATE_____

PRAISE
Write down one praise to the Lord today:

_____

_____

CONFESSION
Write down any sin(s) you need to confess:

_____

_____

THANKSGIVING
Write down what you are most thankful for today:

_____

_____

PETITION
Write down any needs you have in your life today:

_____

_____

INTERCESSION
Write the names of the people you are praying for today and a phrase that expresses your prayer for each person:

Name   Prayer

_____   _____

_____   _____

_____   _____

_____   _____

BIBLE RESPONSE SHEET

DAY/DATE_____

PASSAGE_____

TITLE (Topic of passage) _____

_____

KEY VERSE_____

WHAT DOES IT SAY? (Outline) _____

_____

_____

_____

_____

_____

_____

HOW DOES IT APPLY TO MY LIFE? _____

_____

_____

_____

_____

_____

_____

_____

MEMORIZE VERSE_____

_____

PRAYER ACTION SHEET

DAY/DATE_____

PRAISE
Write down one praise to the Lord today:

_____

_____

CONFESSION
Write down any sin(s) you need to confess:

_____

_____

THANKSGIVING
Write down what you are most thankful for today:

_____

_____

PETITION
Write down any needs you have in your life today:

_____

_____

INTERCESSION
Write the names of the people you are praying for today and a
phrase that expresses your prayer for each person:

Name   Prayer
_____   _____

_____   _____

_____   _____

BIBLE RESPONSE SHEET

DAY/DATE _____

PASSAGE _____

TITLE (Topic of passage) _____

_____

KEY VERSE _____

WHAT DOES IT SAY? (Outline) _____

_____

_____

_____

_____

_____

_____

HOW DOES IT APPLY TO MY LIFE? _____

_____

_____

_____

_____

_____

_____

MEMORIZE VERSE _____

_____

PRAYER ACTION SHEET

DAY/DATE_____

PRAISE
Write down one praise to the Lord today:

_____

_____

CONFESSION
Write down any sin(s) you need to confess:

_____

_____

THANKSGIVING
Write down what you are most thankful for today:

_____

_____

PETITION
Write down any needs you have in your life today:

_____

_____

INTERCESSION
Write the names of the people you are praying for today and a
phrase that expresses your prayer for each person:

Name   Prayer

_____   _____

_____   _____

_____   _____

_____   _____

BIBLE RESPONSE SHEET

DAY/DATE _____

PASSAGE _____

TITLE (Topic of passage) _____

_____

KEY VERSE _____

WHAT DOES IT SAY? (Outline) _____

_____

_____

_____

_____

_____

HOW DOES IT APPLY TO MY LIFE? _____

_____

_____

_____

_____

_____

MEMORIZE VERSE _____

_____

PRAYER ACTION SHEET

DAY/DATE_____

PRAISE
Write down one praise to the Lord today:

_____

_____

CONFESSION
Write down any sin(s) you need to confess:

_____

_____

THANKSGIVING
Write down what you are most thankful for today:

_____

_____

PETITION
Write down any needs you have in your life today:

_____

_____

INTERCESSION
Write the names of the people you are praying for today and a phrase that expresses your prayer for each person:

Name   Prayer

_____   _____

_____   _____

_____   _____

_____   _____

BIBLE RESPONSE SHEET

DAY/DATE_____

PASSAGE_____

TITLE (Topic of passage) _____

_____

KEY VERSE_____

WHAT DOES IT SAY? (Outline) _____

_____

_____

_____

_____

_____

_____

HOW DOES IT APPLY TO MY LIFE? _____

_____

_____

_____

_____

_____

_____

MEMORIZE VERSE_____

_____

PRAYER ACTION SHEET

DAY/DATE _____

PRAISE
Write down one praise to the Lord today:

_____

_____

CONFESSION
Write down any sin(s) you need to confess:

_____

_____

THANKSGIVING
Write down what you are most thankful for today:

_____

_____

PETITION
Write down any needs you have in your life today:

_____

_____

INTERCESSION
Write the names of the people you are praying for today and a phrase that expresses your prayer for each person:

Name   Prayer

_____   _____

_____   _____

_____   _____

_____   _____

BIBLE RESPONSE SHEET

DAY/DATE_____

PASSAGE_____

TITLE (Topic of passage) _____

_____

KEY VERSE_____

WHAT DOES IT SAY? (Outline) _____

_____

_____

_____

_____

_____

_____

HOW DOES IT APPLY TO MY LIFE? _____

_____

_____

_____

_____

_____

_____

_____

MEMORIZE VERSE_____

_____

PRAYER ACTION SHEET

DAY/DATE_____

PRAISE
Write down one praise to the Lord today:

_____

_____

CONFESSION
Write down any sin(s) you need to confess:

_____

_____

THANKSGIVING
Write down what you are most thankful for today:

_____

_____

PETITION
Write down any needs you have in your life today:

_____

_____

INTERCESSION
Write the names of the people you are praying for today and a phrase that expresses your prayer for each person:

Name   Prayer

_____   _____

_____   _____

_____   _____

BIBLE RESPONSE SHEET

DAY/DATE _____

PASSAGE _____

TITLE (Topic of passage) _____

_____

KEY VERSE _____

WHAT DOES IT SAY? (Outline) _____

_____

_____

_____

_____

_____

_____

HOW DOES IT APPLY TO MY LIFE? _____

_____

_____

_____

_____

_____

_____

MEMORIZE VERSE _____

_____

PRAYER ACTION SHEET

DAY/DATE_____

PRAISE
Write down one praise to the Lord today:

_____

_____

CONFESSION
Write down any sin(s) you need to confess:

_____

_____

THANKSGIVING
Write down what you are most thankful for today:

_____

_____

PETITION
Write down any needs you have in your life today:

_____

_____

INTERCESSION
Write the names of the people you are praying for today and a phrase that expresses your prayer for each person:

Name   Prayer

_____   _____

_____   _____

_____   _____

_____   _____

BIBLE RESPONSE SHEET

DAY/DATE _____

PASSAGE _____

TITLE (Topic of passage) _____

_____

KEY VERSE _____

WHAT DOES IT SAY? (Outline) _____

_____

_____

_____

_____

_____

HOW DOES IT APPLY TO MY LIFE? _____

_____

_____

_____

_____

_____

_____

MEMORIZE VERSE _____

_____

PRAYER ACTION SHEET

DAY/DATE_____

PRAISE
Write down one praise to the Lord today:

_____

_____

CONFESSION
Write down any sin(s) you need to confess:

_____

_____

THANKSGIVING
Write down what you are most thankful for today:

_____

_____

PETITION
Write down any needs you have in your life today:

_____

_____

INTERCESSION
Write the names of the people you are praying for today and a phrase that expresses your prayer for each person:

Name   Prayer

_____   _____

_____   _____

_____   _____

_____   _____

BIBLE RESPONSE SHEET

DAY/DATE _____

PASSAGE _____

TITLE (Topic of passage) _____

_____

KEY VERSE _____

WHAT DOES IT SAY? (Outline) _____

_____

_____

_____

_____

_____

HOW DOES IT APPLY TO MY LIFE? _____

_____

_____

_____

_____

_____

_____

MEMORIZE VERSE _____

_____

PRAYER ACTION SHEET

DAY/DATE_____

PRAISE
Write down one praise to the Lord today:

_____

_____

CONFESSION
Write down any sin(s) you need to confess:

_____

_____

THANKSGIVING
Write down what you are most thankful for today:

_____

_____

PETITION
Write down any needs you have in your life today:

_____

_____

INTERCESSION
Write the names of the people you are praying for today and a phrase that expresses your prayer for each person:

Name   Prayer

_____   _____

_____   _____

_____   _____

_____   _____

BIBLE RESPONSE SHEET

DAY/DATE _____

PASSAGE _____

TITLE (Topic of passage) _____

_____

KEY VERSE _____

WHAT DOES IT SAY? (Outline) _____

_____

_____

_____

_____

_____

HOW DOES IT APPLY TO MY LIFE? _____

_____

_____

_____

_____

_____

_____

MEMORIZE VERSE _____

_____

PRAYER ACTION SHEET

DAY/DATE_____

PRAISE
Write down one praise to the Lord today:

_____

_____

CONFESSION
Write down any sin(s) you need to confess:

_____

_____

THANKSGIVING
Write down what you are most thankful for today:

_____

_____

PETITION
Write down any needs you have in your life today:

_____

_____

INTERCESSION
Write the names of the people you are praying for today and a phrase that expresses your prayer for each person:

Name   Prayer

_____   _____

_____   _____

_____   _____

_____   _____

BIBLE RESPONSE SHEET

DAY/DATE _____

PASSAGE _____

TITLE (Topic of passage) _____

_____

KEY VERSE _____

WHAT DOES IT SAY? (Outline) _____

_____

_____

_____

_____

_____

_____

HOW DOES IT APPLY TO MY LIFE? _____

_____

_____

_____

_____

_____

_____

MEMORIZE VERSE _____

_____

PRAYER ACTION SHEET

DAY/DATE_____

PRAISE
Write down one praise to the Lord today:

_____

_____

CONFESSION
Write down any sin(s) you need to confess:

_____

_____

THANKSGIVING
Write down what you are most thankful for today:

_____

_____

PETITION
Write down any needs you have in your life today:

_____

_____

INTERCESSION
Write the names of the people you are praying for today and a phrase that expresses your prayer for each person:

Name   Prayer

_____   _____

_____   _____

_____   _____

_____   _____

BIBLE RESPONSE SHEET

DAY/DATE _____

PASSAGE _____

TITLE (Topic of passage) _____

_____

KEY VERSE _____

WHAT DOES IT SAY? (Outline) _____

_____

_____

_____

_____

_____

_____

HOW DOES IT APPLY TO MY LIFE? _____

_____

_____

_____

_____

_____

_____

_____

MEMORIZE VERSE _____

_____

PRAYER ACTION SHEET

DAY/DATE_____

PRAISE
Write down one praise to the Lord today:

_____

_____

CONFESSION
Write down any sin(s) you need to confess:

_____

_____

THANKSGIVING
Write down what you are most thankful for today:

_____

_____

PETITION
Write down any needs you have in your life today:

_____

_____

INTERCESSION
Write the names of the people you are praying for today and a phrase that expresses your prayer for each person:

Name   Prayer

_____   _____

_____   _____

_____   _____

_____   _____

BIBLE RESPONSE SHEET

DAY/DATE _____

PASSAGE _____

TITLE (Topic of passage) _____

_____

KEY VERSE _____

WHAT DOES IT SAY? (Outline) _____

_____

_____

_____

_____

_____

HOW DOES IT APPLY TO MY LIFE? _____

_____

_____

_____

_____

_____

MEMORIZE VERSE _____

_____

PRAYER ACTION SHEET

DAY/DATE_____

PRAISE
Write down one praise to the Lord today:

_____

_____

CONFESSION
Write down any sin(s) you need to confess:

_____

_____

THANKSGIVING
Write down what you are most thankful for today:

_____

_____

PETITION
Write down any needs you have in your life today:

_____

_____

INTERCESSION
Write the names of the people you are praying for today and a phrase that expresses your prayer for each person:

Name   Prayer

_____   _____

_____   _____

_____   _____

_____   _____

BIBLE RESPONSE SHEET

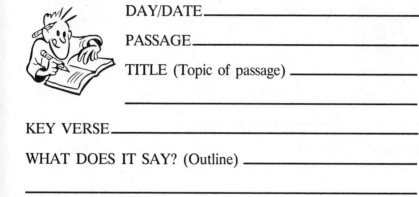

DAY/DATE _____

PASSAGE _____

TITLE (Topic of passage) _____

_____

KEY VERSE _____

WHAT DOES IT SAY? (Outline) _____

_____

_____

_____

_____

_____

HOW DOES IT APPLY TO MY LIFE? _____

_____

_____

_____

_____

_____

MEMORIZE VERSE _____

_____

PRAYER ACTION SHEET

DAY/DATE _____

PRAISE
Write down one praise to the Lord today:

_____

_____

CONFESSION
Write down any sin(s) you need to confess:

_____

_____

THANKSGIVING
Write down what you are most thankful for today:

_____

_____

PETITION
Write down any needs you have in your life today:

_____

_____

INTERCESSION
Write the names of the people you are praying for today and a phrase that expresses your prayer for each person:

Name   Prayer

_____   _____

_____   _____

_____   _____

_____   _____

BIBLE RESPONSE SHEET

DAY/DATE _____

PASSAGE _____

TITLE (Topic of passage) _____

_____

KEY VERSE _____

WHAT DOES IT SAY? (Outline) _____

_____

_____

_____

_____

_____

HOW DOES IT APPLY TO MY LIFE? _____

_____

_____

_____

_____

_____

_____

MEMORIZE VERSE _____

_____

PRAYER ACTION SHEET

DAY/DATE_____

PRAISE
Write down one praise to the Lord today:

_____

_____

CONFESSION
Write down any sin(s) you need to confess:

_____

_____

THANKSGIVING
Write down what you are most thankful for today:

_____

_____

PETITION
Write down any needs you have in your life today:

_____

_____

INTERCESSION
Write the names of the people you are praying for today and a
phrase that expresses your prayer for each person:

Name   Prayer

_____   _____

_____   _____

_____   _____

_____   _____

BIBLE RESPONSE SHEET

DAY/DATE_____

PASSAGE_____

TITLE (Topic of passage) _____

_____

KEY VERSE_____

WHAT DOES IT SAY? (Outline) _____

_____

_____

_____

_____

_____

HOW DOES IT APPLY TO MY LIFE? _____

_____

_____

_____

_____

_____

_____

MEMORIZE VERSE _____

_____

PRAYER ACTION SHEET

DAY/DATE_____

PRAISE
Write down one praise to the Lord today:

_____

_____

CONFESSION
Write down any sin(s) you need to confess:

_____

_____

THANKSGIVING
Write down what you are most thankful for today:

_____

_____

PETITION
Write down any needs you have in your life today:

_____

_____

INTERCESSION
Write the names of the people you are praying for today and a
phrase that expresses your prayer for each person:

Name   Prayer

_____   _____

_____   _____

_____   _____

_____   _____

BIBLE RESPONSE SHEET

DAY/DATE_____

PASSAGE_____

TITLE (Topic of passage) _____

_____

KEY VERSE_____

WHAT DOES IT SAY? (Outline) _____

_____

_____

_____

_____

_____

HOW DOES IT APPLY TO MY LIFE? _____

_____

_____

_____

_____

_____

_____

MEMORIZE VERSE_____

_____

PRAYER ACTION SHEET

DAY/DATE_____

PRAISE
Write down one praise to the Lord today:

_____

_____

CONFESSION
Write down any sin(s) you need to confess:

_____

_____

THANKSGIVING
Write down what you are most thankful for today:

_____

_____

PETITION
Write down any needs you have in your life today:

_____

_____

INTERCESSION
Write the names of the people you are praying for today and a phrase that expresses your prayer for each person:

Name   Prayer

_____   _____

_____   _____

_____   _____

_____   _____

BIBLE RESPONSE SHEET

DAY/DATE _____

PASSAGE _____

TITLE (Topic of passage) _____

_____

KEY VERSE _____

WHAT DOES IT SAY? (Outline) _____

_____

_____

_____

_____

_____

HOW DOES IT APPLY TO MY LIFE? _____

_____

_____

_____

_____

_____

_____

MEMORIZE VERSE _____

_____

PRAYER ACTION SHEET

DAY/DATE_____

PRAISE
Write down one praise to the Lord today:

_____

_____

CONFESSION
Write down any sin(s) you need to confess:

_____

_____

THANKSGIVING
Write down what you are most thankful for today:

_____

_____

PETITION
Write down any needs you have in your life today:

_____

_____

INTERCESSION
Write the names of the people you are praying for today and a phrase that expresses your prayer for each person:

Name   Prayer

_____   _____

_____   _____

_____   _____

_____   _____

BIBLE RESPONSE SHEET

DAY/DATE _____

PASSAGE _____

TITLE (Topic of passage) _____

_____

KEY VERSE _____

WHAT DOES IT SAY? (Outline) _____

_____

_____

_____

_____

_____

_____

HOW DOES IT APPLY TO MY LIFE? _____

_____

_____

_____

_____

_____

_____

MEMORIZE VERSE _____

_____

PRAYER ACTION SHEET

DAY/DATE_____

PRAISE
Write down one praise to the Lord today:

_____

_____

CONFESSION
Write down any sin(s) you need to confess:

_____

_____

THANKSGIVING
Write down what you are most thankful for today:

_____

_____

PETITION
Write down any needs you have in your life today:

_____

_____

INTERCESSION
Write the names of the people you are praying for today and a
phrase that expresses your prayer for each person:

Name   Prayer

_____   _____

_____   _____

_____   _____

_____   _____

BIBLE RESPONSE SHEET

DAY/DATE _____

PASSAGE _____

TITLE (Topic of passage) _____

_____

KEY VERSE _____

WHAT DOES IT SAY? (Outline) _____

_____

_____

_____

_____

_____

_____

HOW DOES IT APPLY TO MY LIFE? _____

_____

_____

_____

_____

_____

_____

_____

MEMORIZE VERSE _____

_____

PRAYER ACTION SHEET

DAY/DATE _____

PRAISE
Write down one praise to the Lord today:

_____

_____

CONFESSION
Write down any sin(s) you need to confess:

_____

_____

THANKSGIVING
Write down what you are most thankful for today:

_____

_____

PETITION
Write down any needs you have in your life today:

_____

_____

INTERCESSION
Write the names of the people you are praying for today and a phrase that expresses your prayer for each person:

Name   Prayer
_____   _____

_____   _____

_____   _____

_____   _____

BIBLE RESPONSE SHEET

DAY/DATE _____

PASSAGE _____

TITLE (Topic of passage) _____

_____

KEY VERSE _____

WHAT DOES IT SAY? (Outline) _____

_____

_____

_____

_____

_____

HOW DOES IT APPLY TO MY LIFE? _____

_____

_____

_____

_____

_____

_____

MEMORIZE VERSE _____

_____

PRAYER ACTION SHEET

DAY/DATE _____

PRAISE
Write down one praise to the Lord today:

_____

_____

CONFESSION
Write down any sin(s) you need to confess:

_____

_____

THANKSGIVING
Write down what you are most thankful for today:

_____

_____

PETITION
Write down any needs you have in your life today:

_____

_____

INTERCESSION
Write the names of the people you are praying for today and a
phrase that expresses your prayer for each person:

Name   Prayer

_____   _____

_____   _____

_____   _____

_____   _____

BIBLE RESPONSE SHEET

DAY/DATE _____

PASSAGE _____

TITLE (Topic of passage) _____

_____

KEY VERSE _____

WHAT DOES IT SAY? (Outline) _____

_____

_____

_____

_____

_____

_____

HOW DOES IT APPLY TO MY LIFE? _____

_____

_____

_____

_____

_____

_____

MEMORIZE VERSE _____

_____

PRAYER ACTION SHEET

DAY/DATE_____

PRAISE
Write down one praise to the Lord today:

_____

_____

CONFESSION
Write down any sin(s) you need to confess:

_____

_____

THANKSGIVING
Write down what you are most thankful for today:

_____

_____

PETITION
Write down any needs you have in your life today:

_____

_____

INTERCESSION
Write the names of the people you are praying for today and a phrase that expresses your prayer for each person:

Name   Prayer

_____   _____

_____   _____

_____   _____

_____   _____

BIBLE RESPONSE SHEET

DAY/DATE _____

PASSAGE _____

TITLE (Topic of passage) _____

_____

KEY VERSE _____

WHAT DOES IT SAY? (Outline) _____

_____

_____

_____

_____

_____

HOW DOES IT APPLY TO MY LIFE? _____

_____

_____

_____

_____

_____

_____

MEMORIZE VERSE _____

_____

PRAYER ACTION SHEET

DAY/DATE_____

PRAISE
Write down one praise to the Lord today:

_____

_____

CONFESSION
Write down any sin(s) you need to confess:

_____

_____

THANKSGIVING
Write down what you are most thankful for today:

_____

_____

PETITION
Write down any needs you have in your life today:

_____

_____

INTERCESSION
Write the names of the people you are praying for today and a phrase that expresses your prayer for each person:

Name   Prayer

_____   _____

_____   _____

_____   _____

_____   _____

BIBLE RESPONSE SHEET

DAY/DATE _____

PASSAGE _____

TITLE (Topic of passage) _____

_____

KEY VERSE _____

WHAT DOES IT SAY? (Outline) _____

_____

_____

_____

_____

_____

HOW DOES IT APPLY TO MY LIFE? _____

_____

_____

_____

_____

_____

_____

_____

MEMORIZE VERSE _____

_____

PRAYER ACTION SHEET

DAY/DATE _____

PRAISE
Write down one praise to the Lord today:

_____

_____

CONFESSION
Write down any sin(s) you need to confess:

_____

_____

THANKSGIVING
Write down what you are most thankful for today:

_____

_____

PETITION
Write down any needs you have in your life today:

_____

_____

INTERCESSION
Write the names of the people you are praying for today and a
phrase that expresses your prayer for each person:

Name   Prayer

_____   _____

_____   _____

_____   _____

_____   _____

BIBLE RESPONSE SHEET

DAY/DATE _____

PASSAGE _____

TITLE (Topic of passage) _____

_____

KEY VERSE _____

WHAT DOES IT SAY? (Outline) _____

_____

_____

_____

_____

_____

_____

HOW DOES IT APPLY TO MY LIFE? _____

_____

_____

_____

_____

_____

_____

MEMORIZE VERSE _____

_____

PRAYER ACTION SHEET

DAY/DATE_____

PRAISE
Write down one praise to the Lord today:

_____

_____

CONFESSION
Write down any sin(s) you need to confess:

_____

_____

THANKSGIVING
Write down what you are most thankful for today:

_____

_____

PETITION
Write down any needs you have in your life today:

_____

_____

INTERCESSION
Write the names of the people you are praying for today and a phrase that expresses your prayer for each person:

Name   Prayer

_____   _____

_____   _____

_____   _____

_____   _____

BIBLE RESPONSE SHEET

DAY/DATE _____

PASSAGE _____

TITLE (Topic of passage) _____

_____

KEY VERSE _____

WHAT DOES IT SAY? (Outline) _____

_____

_____

_____

_____

_____

_____

HOW DOES IT APPLY TO MY LIFE? _____

_____

_____

_____

_____

_____

_____

MEMORIZE VERSE _____

_____

PRAYER ACTION SHEET

DAY/DATE _____

PRAISE
Write down one praise to the Lord today:

_____

_____

CONFESSION
Write down any sin(s) you need to confess:

_____

_____

THANKSGIVING
Write down what you are most thankful for today:

_____

_____

PETITION
Write down any needs you have in your life today:

_____

_____

INTERCESSION
Write the names of the people you are praying for today and a phrase that expresses your prayer for each person:

Name   Prayer

_____   _____

_____   _____

_____   _____

_____   _____

BIBLE RESPONSE SHEET

DAY/DATE _____

PASSAGE _____

TITLE (Topic of passage) _____

_____

KEY VERSE _____

WHAT DOES IT SAY? (Outline) _____

_____

_____

_____

_____

_____

_____

HOW DOES IT APPLY TO MY LIFE? _____

_____

_____

_____

_____

_____

_____

MEMORIZE VERSE _____

_____

PRAYER ACTION SHEET

DAY/DATE_____

PRAISE
Write down one praise to the Lord today:

_____

_____

CONFESSION
Write down any sin(s) you need to confess:

_____

_____

THANKSGIVING
Write down what you are most thankful for today:

_____

_____

PETITION
Write down any needs you have in your life today:

_____

_____

INTERCESSION
Write the names of the people you are praying for today and a phrase that expresses your prayer for each person:

Name   Prayer

_____   _____

_____   _____

_____   _____

_____   _____

BIBLE RESPONSE SHEET

DAY/DATE _____

PASSAGE _____

TITLE (Topic of passage) _____

_____

KEY VERSE _____

WHAT DOES IT SAY? (Outline) _____

_____

_____

_____

_____

_____

HOW DOES IT APPLY TO MY LIFE? _____

_____

_____

_____

_____

_____

_____

MEMORIZE VERSE _____

_____

PRAYER ACTION SHEET

DAY/DATE_____

PRAISE
Write down one praise to the Lord today:

_____

_____

CONFESSION
Write down any sin(s) you need to confess:

_____

_____

THANKSGIVING
Write down what you are most thankful for today:

_____

_____

PETITION
Write down any needs you have in your life today:

_____

_____

INTERCESSION
Write the names of the people you are praying for today and a phrase that expresses your prayer for each person:

Name   Prayer

_____   _____

_____   _____

_____   _____

BIBLE RESPONSE SHEET

DAY/DATE _____

PASSAGE _____

TITLE (Topic of passage) _____

_____

KEY VERSE _____

WHAT DOES IT SAY? (Outline) _____

_____

_____

_____

_____

_____

_____

HOW DOES IT APPLY TO MY LIFE? _____

_____

_____

_____

_____

_____

_____

_____

MEMORIZE VERSE _____

_____

PRAYER ACTION SHEET

DAY/DATE _____

PRAISE
Write down one praise to the Lord today:

_____

_____

CONFESSION
Write down any sin(s) you need to confess:

_____

_____

THANKSGIVING
Write down what you are most thankful for today:

_____

_____

PETITION
Write down any needs you have in your life today:

_____

_____

INTERCESSION
Write the names of the people you are praying for today and a phrase that expresses your prayer for each person:

Name   Prayer

_____   _____

_____   _____

_____   _____

_____   _____

BIBLE RESPONSE SHEET

DAY/DATE _____

PASSAGE _____

TITLE (Topic of passage) _____

_____

KEY VERSE _____

WHAT DOES IT SAY? (Outline) _____

_____

_____

_____

_____

_____

HOW DOES IT APPLY TO MY LIFE? _____

_____

_____

_____

_____

_____

_____

MEMORIZE VERSE _____

_____

PRAYER ACTION SHEET

DAY/DATE _____

PRAISE
Write down one praise to the Lord today:

_____

_____

CONFESSION
Write down any sin(s) you need to confess:

_____

_____

THANKSGIVING
Write down what you are most thankful for today:

_____

_____

PETITION
Write down any needs you have in your life today:

_____

_____

INTERCESSION
Write the names of the people you are praying for today and a
phrase that expresses your prayer for each person:

Name   Prayer

_____   _____

_____   _____

_____   _____

_____   _____

NOTES

NOTES

NOTES

NOTES

NOTES

NOTES

NOTES

NOTES

NOTES

NOTES

NOTES

NOTES

NOTES

NOTES

NOTES

NOTES